D1085183

THE WALTER LYNWOOD FLEMING
LECTURES IN SOUTHERN HISTORY
*Louisiana State University*

Another Look at the
Twentieth-Century South

# Another Look at the Twentieth-Century South

## GEORGE E. MOWRY

LOUISIANA STATE UNIVERSITY PRESS
BATON ROUGE

ISBN 0–8071–0230–X
Library of Congress Catalog Card Number 72–83037
Copyright © 1973 by Louisiana State University Press
All rights reserved
Manufactured in the United States of America
Printed by Kingsport Press, Inc., Kingsport, Tennessee
Designed by Albert R. Crochet

time exhibit my growing slothfulness in not honor-
ing just debts with the usual footnotes.

The lack of emphasis in this volume on the black
man may be remarked upon since so patently he has
left his mark upon the entirety of southern history.
Actually, however, if the Negro is rarely mentioned
in this little work, he is obviously the major presence offstage. His abstraction from the first chapter
proves, I think, the point. For if my thesis here is
supportable, southern history without the black
would have been very little different from that of
the western Middle West. And if in the two concluding chapters, devoted to an examination of the
southern political and economic elite, the black
voice is practically mute and the poor white's barely
audible on matters of public policy, this signifies little about their respective contributions in the shaping of total southern culture. One final comment
upon the implications of this study for the racial
issue. Only the most zealous materialist would care
to argue that the larger question of race in the
South was and is exclusively economic in nature.
But in the realm of American public policy, a be-
wildering complex of human feelings and thought
is often hidden in and simplified by a prosaic vote
on appropriations, or by a statement on desirable
wage levels. And as public expressions of traditional racial views have become discredited, the in-

clination to euphemize them has apparently increased.

My thanks are due to the staff on the Louisiana State University Press, who greatly aided in the conversion of a messy lecture manuscript into something which is, I hope, fit for print. Lastly I would like to pay tribute to one reader, unknown to me, for his many helpful comments and suggestions which improved the work considerably and saved the author from a number of embarrassing errors.

# Contents

Another Look at the
Twentieth-Century South

# I

## The Twentieth-Century South:
## A Comparative View

One of the most astonishing things about southern
history is the amount of it taught and written in
southern institutions of learning. Few such institutions are so small that they do not include at least
one historian of the South on their faculty, and
most of them have a collection of scholars whose
primary research and teaching interest is centered
on the region. Probably no other section of history
is so intensively covered in the classroom, and certainly no other section has produced so many mono-
graphs and books about its past. The distinguished
ten-volume *History of the South* produced by the
Louisiana State University Press is unmatched anywhere in the United States in either the intensity
of its coverage or the parochialism of its interest.

Numerous historical studies exist, of course, on
New England and the middle states and again on
the West, but there is no unified history of the

North. Except for history of a peculiar antiquarian flavor, few attempts have been made at western regional scholarship in more recent times. Some regional historical societies do exist, but since the old Mississippi Valley Historical Association added the subtitle a *Journal of American History* to its quarterly in 1939, reflecting a development that years before had taken place in its contents, there has been no regional historical society or journal thereof which has either enrolled the members or exerted the influence of the Southern Historical Association and its *Journal of Southern History*. Although the Southern's meetings have strayed somewhat from its primary purpose of depicting southern life and culture, a cursory review of recent numbers of its journal will indicate that the magazine steadfastly persists in its obvious determination to confine itself to southern subjects.

I assume that for a society to originate and grow as the Southern Historical Association has done, many of its participating members have to be inspired with the feelings that the organization is needed to fill some personal and academic gap and that the subject is both important and unique. And certainly if there seems to be one feeling that justifies most recent historians of the South in their efforts, it is the singularity of their subject. As always in the historical fraternity there is a contrapuntal opinion. In numerous essays David Potter has warned of the fallacy inherent in treating southern history as entirely distinct from that of the nation. George Tindall and Charles Sellers, among others, have also stressed the common forces at work in both national and southern history; and Howard Zinn, writing from the New Left position, states that far from being singular, southern history has reflected "in concentrated and dangerous form a set of characteristics which mark the country as a whole."

Minority voices aside, however, the insistent chorus of most scholars writing about the recent South has been keyed to the fundamental assumption that the section, at least for the day before yesterday, to use C. Vann Woodward's phrase, has been unique among the regions of the country. Thus with some qualifications Woodward speaks of "the eccentric position" of the South in the nation, and Frank Vandiver writes of "the southern difference." Dewey Grantham characterizes the region as the "most stubbornly sectional, and the most aberrant from national norms," and V. O. Key, Jr., refers to the section's "variant political activities." Louis Hartz calls the South "an alien child" in the national family, and even Charles Sellers, in his preface to *The Southerner as American*, refers to the section's "essential southernism."

5

The search among southern historians for the "central theme" of southern history, or, on another level, the "true essence of southern identity" reflects the same outlook, both quests being based upon the assumption that southern history has a central theme different from that or those of the rest of the nation and a sectional identity separable and distinguishable from it.

In proof of the particularity of the South, recent southern historians have offered many explanations. Among the more important of these is the almost universally mentioned factor of race, a concept including both the Negro minority and the Anglo-Saxon or British majority which is invariably described as the most homogenous class of its kind in the country. The monolithic Protestantism of the South, especially its Baptist and Methodist sects, is also usually cited, thus making the Southerner the archetype WASP—white Anglo-Saxon Protestant. Key, concerned almost entirely with politics, ascribes much of the southern difference to the peculiar one-party system of the section and the pervasive conservatism flowing from it. Walter Prescott Webb, interested in the economics of sectionalism, found, in 1937 at least, the region's colonial status to be the explanation for most of its ills and differences. Leslie W. Dunbar has isolated the southern folk—"clearly, if not definable, more a single people than any other Americans"—as the major determinant of the region's particularism. Robert Penn Warren, the novelist, has ascribed the psychological heritage of the Civil War as the controlling factor giving the South "a great alibi" and the North a "treasury of virtue," psychological concepts to which both sections have been reacting ever since. Other motor forces in shaping the South's peculiar mentality are listed by various authors to be the region's climate, its propensity for violence, its lack of education, and the high incidence of malaria, yellow fever, and hookworm. Finally, in a kind of an overview, C. Vann Woodward published in 1960 his impressive *The Burden of Southern History*, in which he argued that the real serpent in the southern Eden and the forces that set it apart from the rest of the nation were, in essence, its history whose controlling and separable elements were compounded of poverty, failure, guilt, and tragedy to an extent unexperienced by the remainder of the country.

Whatever their individual weight, the collective burden of these three chapters is to examine these generalizations about the recent South. For a nonsoutherner and especially a nonsouthern historian to challenge the consensus of so many distinguished scholars is perhaps foolhardy. And if I seem to be joining mad dogs and Englishmen in a rush for the revealing noonday sun, instead of more properly sequestering myself in a darkened library carrell looking up more facts, I ask forebearance, and plead to having been led into this precarious path by a couple of recent interests in comparative history and American conservatism. The more I looked into these areas with particular reference to the recent South the more I was puzzled by the seeming gap between the record and the historical generalizations of the authorities. As a result, in the first chapter I examine recent southern history from a comparative viewpoint. In the second I will inquire into recent southern conservatism, and in the third, I will attempt to suggest the two main objectives of the power elite in the South which on the whole have been successfully realized and which perhaps constitute major themes of twentieth-century southern history.

History as an unlimited grab bag of varied events, ideas, and customs, in which a student can find at least a few examples of anything he originally sets out to seek, is a commonplace experience of researchers. For every generalization made about masses of people in large areas, multitudinous exceptions always exist, and especially with unquantifiable things the researcher's predilections and methods are often the main determinative of his findings. In comparative history the choice of what is to be compared is also a major factor in the final result. A comparison, for example, of the people of the states of New York and Illinois might lead to one series of conclusions, a second between the inhabitants of New York City and Chicago another, and or a not always conscious purpose, a comparer can choose to stress either likenesses or differences. Since most southern historians have chosen to emphasize the differences between their section and the rest of the nation, I frankly have looked for similarities and thus have sought a section not too different from the South in its social, economic, and political dimensions. Considering my starting date of 1900, it was immediately apparent that the other section should not be the industrialized and urbanized Northeast, almost invariably selected in the past, but should be a portion of the Middle West that was most agrarian, and one raising agricultural staples for export. By those injunctions the obvious choice had to be that portion of the Middle West lying to the Pacific side of the Mississippi River and the Atlantic side of the high plains, an area usually designated as the western Middle West.

Generally comparing the physical and demographic qualities of the two regions, one readily thinks of the climate and the availability of water and woodlands as differentiating factors, but in most other aspects the seven states of Minnesota, Iowa, Missouri, North and South Dakota, Kansas, and Nebraska show a remarkable similarity to the region comprising the Old Confederacy. While the southern region was considerably larger in area, by perhaps 40 to 50 percent, it also contained more than twice the population. Consequently the important land-to-man factor was roughly equivalent in both sectors until 1940. After that date, however, whereas the southern population continued to grow rapidly, that of the western Middle West was stagnant and in some cases actually declined, so that by 1950 the population of the southern region was almost triple that of the western Middle West. Until 1930 the agrarian-urban balance in the two sections was also remarkably equivalent. The South in 1910 had no metropolitan center to rival St. Louis' almost seven hundred thousand people. But New Orleans at that time was larger than Minneapolis, and Birmingham was greater in population than Omaha. Since 1940, of course, the urbanization of the South has proceeded far more rapidly than that of the western Middle West.

In discussing the national origins or the racial composition of the people of the two sections, the problem of the Negro is an obviously difficult one, but since southern historians have repeatedly excluded that race when talking about the remarkable

In religious affiliations the census reports reflect an amazing coincidence between the two sections throughout much of the twentieth century. In 1900 both were overwhelmingly Protestant, and both still are except in the very large cities and in scattered rural areas. In 1970 the Roman Catholic Church reported almost twice the number of communicants living in the states of the Old Confederacy than in those of the western Middle West, four and one-half against two and seven-tenths millions, and even in the cities the ratios are not too unequivalent. About the same number of Catholics, for example, live in Little Rock, Arkansas, as in Lincoln, Nebraska. Granted, there are fewer Baptists and more Lutherans in the western Middle West, but except for variant stands on cardplaying and the consumption of alcohol, the moral and social ethics emanating from both churches have been approximately the same. Studies of the social gospel disseminated from the pulpits during the early years of the twentieth century indicate that it was almost nil in both sections, and it might boggle that mind forced to decide which were the most orthodox in theology, the southern Baptists or the Lutherans of the Missouri synod. From such evidence one is forced to conclude that both the South and the western Middle West were the citadels par excellence of the WASP.

In 1937 Professor Walter Prescott Webb published his *Divided We Stand*, a book that attracted national attention with its thesis that the United States was marked by three cultures: an industrial and financial one in the Northeast and two agricultural and extractive ones in the South and the West. Each culture, Webb argued, was separate and recognizable. Central to the Texan's argument was his opinion, bolstered throughout the book by a plenitude of statistics, that the South and the West were economic satellites to the Northeast, made so in the first instance by the developments of the Civil War and subsequently perpetuated by unequal pensions, freight rates, capital, and interest charges.

A year later, perhaps more for reasons of politics than sectional justice, Franklin Roosevelt called the South "the nation's economic problem number one." Subsequently politicians of both sections, Governor Ellis Arnall of Georgia and Senator Patrick McCarren of Nevada, for example, argued zealously that long-continued, politically inspired disadvantages were primarily responsible for their own sections' slow economic development. Recent historians have picked up this theme of section discrimination in order to help explain the South's unique mentality. C. Vann Woodward includes poverty prominently among the burdens of southern history. "The history of the South," he states, "includes a long and quite un-American experience with poverty." Dewey Grantham, Frank Vandiver, and Frank Freidel agree with Woodward that the section's "frustration, failure, and defeat," as contrasted with the general American success story, have played a major part in the conditioning of the southern mind.

After the post-World War II burgeoning of the Texas economy, Professor Webb recanted many of his strictures, but if taken in gross and measured against the national average, his and Roosevelt's conclusion about the relative economic standards in the South appear to be correct, at least for the depression years. However, when southern distress is measured against that of the western Middle West, the disparity suffered by the South is small indeed. Nine-cent cotton from 1931 to 1935 was matched by sixty-cent wheat, and though the corn and dairy belt of the western Middle West fared somewhat better, government statistics for the two sections indicate no large discrepancy in gross income payments except between the richer states, Minnesota and Iowa, and the more economically backward states, Alabama and Mississippi. During the thirties both black and white marginal farmers left their southern fields just as did the equally marginal producers of the wheat lands. The wheat farmers were then being assaulted by dust storms and drought as well as by starvation prices. Californians called them "Oakies" although a good proportion of them came from the Dakotas, western Nebraska and Kansas, as well as Oklahoma.

Webb's own figures dealing with time deposits and banking and checking accounts in banks, income tax payments, and corporate profits, indicate that there was little choice between the economy of the South and of the West, both being monumentally overshadowed by that of the Northeast. By 1940, according to the statistics of the Department of Commerce, personal income in the South Atlantic states amounted to $459 per capita against $483 for the western North Central states. But even such close gross figures obscure another important factor in assaying relative sectional incomes. Every available statistic gathered before 1960 indicates the great discrepancy in yearly income between the blacks and the white men in the South. Consequently, gross averages importantly minimize white income and maximize those for the blacks. Since the black percentage of the 1940 population ran anywhere between 50 percent in Mississippi to 31 percent in North Carolina and a microscopic figure for the western Middle West, this distortion factor becomes important enough to warrant the supposition that in a large part of the South, the average white man was at least as well off as those in the western

Middle West, and the white upper economic classes substantially so.

Overall regional figures comparing white and black incomes for the period are extremely difficult to obtain, but what figures do exist indicate that the yearly income of blacks might well have been anywhere from 40 to 60 percent of that of the white, making this distortion factor weigh heaviest in precisely the poorest states of the South.

To summarize, the southern Negro along with the urban unemployed was obviously the nation's number one economic problem during the depression. And the poor, white, landless Southerner may well have been in the second place. But as far as the southern whites as a whole were concerned, their economic condition was apparently better than that of their fellows in the western Middle West. Therefore, poverty resulting from the Civil War invasion and defeat may well have partially explained the southern psyche immediately following Reconstruction; during the twentieth century it was obviously no more a conditioning factor than in the farming country lying west of the Mississippi River.

In an article entitled "The Search for Southern Identity," C. Vann Woodward includes one-party politics as one of the several peculiarities that offered "indisputable proof that the South was different." Professor Key agrees that both the institution of one-party control and its conservative results have marked the section as aberrant from national norms, and although Dewey Grantham in *The Democratic South* has emphasized the amount of southern progressive action, he also writes in the same volume that the South's loyalty to the Democratic Party is the "most remarkable phenomenon" of its kind in American history. From such conclusions southern historians have argued that a long list of deleterious political results have followed, among them the dominance of the Confederate military tradition, a pervasive conservatism, the irresponsibility of the Bourbon politicians, the control of local politics by courthouse rings, low wages engineered by right-to-work laws, a proliferation of demagogues and primarily the suppression of the Negro, one of the main objects of one-party control. Except for the central statement that one-party politics was a near monopoly of the South and therefore a talisman of the section's uniqueness, there is of course some truth in all of these remarks. But a comparison of southern and western middle western political history will, I think, support the statement that the South was not unique in its political institutions or in the results flowing from them.

As Dewey Grantham has shown, the South was scarcely a one-party section before 1900. Nor has it been in the twentieth century except for the first

17

twenty years when the disfranchisement of the Negro gave the section a solidly, if transitory, Democratic cast. But Tennessee elected a Republican governor before 1920, and with Harding's election Republicanism again began to wax, reaching a peak in 1928, when the entire upper South supported Hoover. Between 1930 and 1936 the South was overwhelmingly Democratic, as was the rest of the nation. But with the attempt a year later by three Democratic southern senators to form a conservative coalition against the New Deal, the South's loyalty to the Democratic Party was again in question. The war submerged this dissidence but did not destroy it, and, in fact, the amazing postwar developments of modern Republicanism in the South and the growth of state independent Democratic parties often at odds with the national organization, together with third-party candidates, can all be dated from 1937.

In its allegiance to one-party politics in national elections, the record of the western Middle West, especially in the period after 1900, was not too dissimilar to that of the South. Bryan carried Nebraska in 1908, and Wilson in 1912 and 1916 won the electoral votes of most of the corn and wheat belt states. But it is interesting to note that in 1912 Wilson failed to get a majority of the popular votes in any of the western middle western states. Mean-

disrupted conventional politics in both sections. Much to the point here is the record of successful Republican candidates for the Presidency. Every one from Hayes through Harrison was a bearded Union officer. With the pension issue exciting extra enthusiasm, one might guess that the northern campaign plea "vote the way you shot," elicited as much response as did the counter-exhortations to the South. Certainly the so-called southern Redeemers and Bourbons, after they had gained power in their states, showed little sense of public responsibility when confronted with the possibilities of enormous private gain through the manipulation of public lands and private railroads. Certainly on the local level southern politics was controlled by courthouse rings made up of planters, merchants, and lawyers. But can anything better be said about the distribution of public lands and the greed of the railroad operators throughout the western Middle West? It should be remembered that the more notorious of the robber barons and their latter-day descendants operated to the north and to the west; likewise in more local settings, the attorneys for railroads, lumber interests, and meat packers were often as dominant in local politics as were their southern cohorts. Their control of local politics in the interests of themselves, their principals, and the upper economic classes in general operated just as it did

not at all sure that I know what that word means, unless it applies to a successful politician who fervently appeals to the masses for ends with which one does not agree and by methods not considered cricket by one's own associates. John Adams, for example, distinguished between "aristocratical" and "democratical" demagogues. If one assumes that such a definition is reasonably correct, then I would suggest that almost as many demagogues, so labeled by their opponents, have appeared in the Middle West as in the South. To name a few, Ignatius Donnelly, Mary Lease, Sockless Jerry Simpson, Coin Harvey, William Jennings Bryan, most of the successful progressive leaders in the western Middle West, the Non-Partisan Leaguers in the Dakotas and Minnesota, the Sons of the Wild Jackasses, as the farm-bloc leaders were called by Senator George H. Moses in the twenties, and Senator Joseph McCarthy of Wisconsin. All of these men were called demagogues by their opponents, especially during the time they effectively threatened the reigning economic or social establishment. The derogatory term, of course, has persisted more with reference to southern politicians like Hoke Smith and Tom Watson of Georgia, Vardaman and Bilbo of Mississippi, Long of Louisiana, but one is certain that in most cases the term was used because of their stand on race, which excited the emotions of both northeastern conservatives and liberals. And as the center of the publishing, the broadcasting, and the television industries, the Northeast has had a predominant role in deciding what goes into the permanent national record. To the point is the fact that except for the race question, which La Follette never had to face in his home constituency, the ideological careers of Vardaman and La Follette, one the champion of the Mississippi rednecks and the other of the one-gallused farmer of Wisconsin, were strikingly similar. Both were progressive, reforming governors, both took their reform crusades into the Senate, both were vehement opponents of intervention into World War I, and both were labeled demagogues by the representatives of the reigning economic and social classes of their own states. Now La Follette is considered a statesman, and Vardaman often depicted as a rabble-rouser.

One of the recurring assumptions of southern literary and political historians is that there was and is an easily separate and identifiable southern people. Cash's *Mind of the South* is obviously premised on such an assumption. Such diverse persons as the political scientist Leslie W. Dunbar, the critic Allen Tate, the novelist Robert Penn Warren, and historians David Potter, Frank Vandiver, and C. Vann Woodward all agree. Dunbar states flatly, "There has been such a thing as a southern folk, clearly, if not definably, more a single people than any other Americans." Vandiver writes, "It is easy to tell a southerner," and asks if that could be said of any other Americans. From the postulation of a southern folk, there follows an assumption that there is a southern mind, and southern historians have not been bashful about analyzing the separate qualities of that mind. Thus Cash attributes to the southern upper-class mentality a long list of virtues and faults, including bravery, pride, honor, courtesy, generosity, loyalty on the one hand, and on the other an inclination to violence, intolerance and suspicion toward new ideas, an incapacity for analysis, and an exaggerated individualism. Vandiver emphasizes violence, hot temper, and an inclination to quick resentment, as coming from the land, climate, and blood. Woodward expresses the more somber attributes originating from a pervasive sectional pessimism concerned with a sense of guilt and an acknowledgment of evil. With their multitude of facets, such things as folk cultures and folk minds are extremely difficult to measure, to say nothing of arriving at comparative judgments. More often than not, the final judgment is based upon the mentality of the viewer, rather than upon that of the viewed, upon the viewer's own selection of materials, actual experience, upon the context of his argument, and upon the purposes to which it is being put. All of these, of course, are appropriate to the present argument, and I must frankly state that I have read far more so-called folk literature from the Middle West than from the South, and my own actual experience in the small middle western community is approximately double in length my similar residence in the South. But granting these limitations and the reliability of memory, I can remember few influential peculiarities in either the folk or folk culture of either section. Obvious, unimportant differences did exist. In the western Middle West one missed the smell of wood smoke and the hot pines in the summer and the sight of Negroes. The pronunciation, cadence, and the thrust of language varied somewhat between the sections. But southern speech was as fully understandable in the Middle West as was that of the Middle West in the South. There existed no startling variance of comprehension as exists even today between the humble folk of Yorkshire and Sussex in England, to say nothing of Wales and Scotland. In the twenties there were obviously far more tractors in the fields of Iowa and fewer horses and mules than in North Carolina or Mississippi. The rich in the South appeared to be richer, the poor, poorer. But on the whole, as one drove into a small courthouse town— and I am assuming that the small town is the maker as well as the conservator of folk culture—one saw few differences between a southern and middle western town of approximately the same size. The same ugly Methodist and Baptist churches dominated the community, and if they had been built in the twenties, they were often of yellow brick in the American factory style of church architecture. One sat down in much the same sort of café and was greeted with the same kind of loquacity in tones ranging from congenial to real warmth, both tones contrasting with the almost standard reticence equated with efficiency in the more northeasterly parts of the nation. When the food arrived in southern or northern café, it was usually cooked to death, and the entire experience contained about as much significant variation as the difference between midwestern hominy and southern grits.

If one stayed in town longer than overnight, one observed the folkways of the southern and trans-Mississippi small town of five to ten thousand varied little. The town was run by a courthouse clique made up of lawyers, officials, and hangerson. But almost every important matter was not finally settled until the banker, drygoods merchant, and newspaper owner had been consulted. Laws, especially "blue laws," were strict on paper, but the enforcement was selective rather than fortuitous. At one time, Kansas was the only state in the Union to have on its books an anti-cigarette law, and it was one of the last to forsake legally the Anti-Saloon League. In Kansas as in Mississippi, although the bum found with an illegal half pint by the railroad tracks was given three days and a vigorous invitation to leave the town thereafter, the country club, the American Legion, the Benevolent Order of Elks were much more hospitably treated. Both states were able to provide illegal gambling devices as well as a good liquor solace to the unhappy loser. From the weekly newspaper as well as from the Sunday sermon, country and town folk got a straight dose of the Protestant ethic. Complete strangers staying in town for any time were looked upon with a maximum of suspicion, and if a man's mission was not spelled out clearly, the outsider would be usually designated by the community as a probable agitator, which meant, more often than not, a union organizer. Altogether it was a remarkably similar experience that the country man or small towner found in either of the sections.

To measure the past mind of an entire section is an almost impossible task for the historian, and it is indeed doubtful whether a section can properly be said to have a *mind*. For all of their precision tools, modern samplers of public opinion are decidedly given to error even on simple questions, and the sharp differences of opinion from group to group and equally from time to time should indicate

27

to us the fallibility inherent in talking about the complex feelings of men of past eras, and in particular about such subtleties as their depth of pessimism, sense of tragedy, and intensity of guilt feelings. Up to now at least, I think it can be fairly said, the usual historical judgment on such points has been a highly personal one based on a subjective judgment of chaotic samplings of records preserved by intellectuals, politicians, preachers, and other literate groups. The evident gap during the past forty or fifty years between the mentality of the intellectuals and that of the American masses should warn us not to impute too close a relationship in their thinking during that period.

Even with these precautionary statements in mind, on first reading it is seemingly true, as C. Vann Woodward points out, that the gospel of progress which flourished north of Mason and Dixon's line in the nineteenth century "never found wide acceptance below the Potomac. . . ." Woodward cites in evidence for the generalization the hopeful writings emanating from the North, the confidence of northern businessmen, the flowering of many utopian schemes in that section. In comparison he states that the South's preoccupation was with guilt, not with innocence, with the reality of evil and not perfection. It should be pointed out here that Woodward is concerned with the Northeast and not

status of the region. But even more qualification needs to be made in Woodward's statements if one looks particularly at the western Middle West. Overall, except for extraordinary times, agricultural sections have never been too sanguine, and the record of the western Middle West in the nineteenth century was never too hopeful, either in its political or literary manifestations. The records of the Greenbackers, the antimonopolites, the Grangers, and the Populists were filled with a recounting of the disasters of the past and forebodings of the future. So also, was the tone of the literature coming from the section. Hamlin Garland and O. E. Rolvaag and Willa Cather are not exactly purveyors of cheer concerning man's basic nature or the future of agriculture. Assuredly, most of their heroes testified to the triumph of the human spirit over implacable natural and human enemies, but a later generation of middle western writers with agricultural or small-town backgrounds, peopled their books with the infinitely diminished creatures of Evansville, Indiana, and Winesburg, Ohio, and Sauk City, Minnesota. Louis D. Rubin, Jr., has explicitly made the point that it was not "southern local color that Wolfe and Faulkner studied"; it was the works of Theodore Dreiser, Sherwood Anderson, and Sinclair Lewis. Consequently, despite the argument of Allen Tate and other recent southern literary critics that recent southern literature is unique, it is not surprising to find the literature of the two sections permeated with much of the same spirit and containing a good many parallels in character and incident.

In concluding this hasty Cook's tour of two major sections of the country, I would suggest that up until World War II, at least, the South and the western Middle West were alike in many significant ways. Substantial differences did exist, of course, the most important of which unquestionably was the presence of sizable numbers of black people in every southern state. Directly connected with the racial mixture in the South was the apparent sharp inequality of income distribution. A third varying factor, not hitherto mentioned, consisted of the political behavior of the southern conservative elite which contrasted sharply with that in the western Middle West. These three southern elements, I would argue, are closely interrelated, and together they illuminate the course of recent southern history as do few others whether of historic, romantic, psychic, or material origin.

# II

## The Paradox of
## Southern Conservatism

*Conservatism* is one of the slipperiest words in the English language and as applied to twentieth-century America alone its explication would require more than three chapters. I would like to use a rough definition of the word as that state of mind inclined to defend the status quo and exhibiting most of the other characteristics so well outlined by Clinton Rossiter in his brilliant little volume, *Conservatism in America*.

This rather general definition has been used, I believe, by most of the scholars writing about the recent South. With a few exceptions they have arrived at Rossiter's conclusion that "the South has always been the most conservative area in the United States." This offhand judgment has been sustained by the detailed work of Rossiter's fellow political scientist, V. O. Key, Jr., who while lamenting that "the South ought, by all rules of political behavior, to be radical," then proceeds to assert, by an examination of local and state politics, that the region has been dominated by an abiding conservatism. Most other types of scholars, including the historians, have agreed. Cash, the journalist, and Rubin, the literary critic, have called the section "profoundly conservative." The historian Frank Freidel has entitled an essay on the South and the New Deal as "The Conservative South." Dewey Grantham, who, along with C. Vann Woodward, has done most to acquaint the public with the persistent Populist-Progressive reform impulse in the section, has concluded that despite all the acids of modernity, the section's "basic ideas remain fundamentally conservative." Though conceding that the South was born Lockean in its political philosophy, Vann Woodward has concluded that it grew to be "an alien child in a liberal family, tortured and confused, driven to a fantasy life."

A few southern historians, most of them, significantly, scholars of the twentieth century, have raised objections to these conclusions. Focusing not on the section's local affairs but rather upon its representation in Washington during the Wilson years, Arthur Link has come to a different conclusion, and George Tindall, challenging the thesis of the area's "monolithic conservatism," has assigned the proposition to the realm of "southern mythology." But the vast majority of scholars, a few with pride, but most with despair, concur in the consensus that the South has been and still remains in the conservative rear guard of American politics.

I have neither the inclination nor the detailed knowledge to challenge extensively this thesis in the area of local and state politics, although I am sure that the record of many southern states would not be too different from those in the western Middle West. In subjecting the intensity of southern conservatism to analysis, I would like to shift the focus from local regions to the national scene, not only for the years of Wilson's New Freedom as Link has done, but for the first fifty years of the twentieth century, and more particularly to three periods of national control by the Democratic Party, years which coincided with three specific reform programs well known as the New Freedom, the New Deal and the Fair Deal. Why only the periods of Democratic control? Largely because minorities are notorious for the consistency of their efforts to embarrass the majority at whatever cost either to the nation or to their own considered convictions. Secondly, because since 1912 the periods of liberal radical or creative politics—call them what you will—have been identical with Democratic incumbency of the Presidency. Judged by their legislative programs, no Democratic conservative has been

elected President in the twentieth century. Consequently during these periods the so-called southern
conservatives had to place their votes where their
mouths were not or be branded party defectors.

More specifically, within these three reform periods I would like to look closely at the record of
three southern senators as representatives of the
so-called conservative South: John Sharp Williams
of Mississippi, Josiah W. Bailey of North Carolina,
and James F. Byrnes of South Carolina. I chose
senators because they represent entire states and
because their voting and their verbal records are
far more available than those of representatives.

The question of why I selected these particular
three is a valid one. Many others might have been
chosen, for example, Carter Glass and Harry Flood
Byrd of Virginia, Walter F. George of Georgia,
Oscar W. Underwood and William B. Bankhead of
Alabama, and Pat Harrison of Mississippi. But I
wanted a spread in class or social origins as well
as in time spent in the Senate. Moreover, the three
men selected either have written their own works
or have been written about extensively. Williams
and Bailey have attracted respectable scholarly bi-
ographers, and at least two perceptive theses have
already been written on Byrnes. The recent historian has to position any comprehensive synthetic
work on that by others in the hope that even a

pygmy can see farther than a giant if he stands upon the giant's shoulders.

From the character of its leadership as well as its announced program, the Wilson administration can be described as the first southern dominated one since before the Civil War. Wilson himself was a southerner, born and schooled in the section. Both his personal political ideology and his campaign rhetoric were thoroughly acceptable to a great many southerners. In the election Wilson secured a majority vote in only one state north of Mason and Dixon's line, but from Virginia to Texas the Old Confederacy gave him solid support.

Wilson acknowledged the geographical character of his popularity by his important appointments. Five of his cabinet were southern born. Two of his more important advisers, Edward M. House and Bernard Baruch were born in the South. The Wilsonian establishment in both Houses of Congress was probably more southern in its makeup than in any administration before or since. In the House the Speaker, the majority floor leader, and thirteen of the sixteen important committee chairmen were Southerners by birth. The comparable figures for the Senate were ten of fourteen. Obviously, Wilson could have achieved no consequential legislation during his first term without southern concurrence and indeed active support. In terms of personal ideology of the House and Senate leadership this meant conservative support, and the President freely acknowledged its nature. His head, he told his secretary in 1914, was with the progressive Democrats, but his heart was with the "the Old Guard in the Senate" because of the way they had stood by him in almost every critical vote.

John Sharp Williams was not one of the more important establishmentarians of the Senate, although as the former Democratic House minority leader he was made in 1911 a member of both the powerful Finance and Foreign Relations committees. And in most ways he exemplified the traditional southern conservative's consistent support for Wilson's domestic program even though the New Freedom grew increasingly liberal as it unfolded.

Born in Memphis in 1854 but raised on a Black Belt cotton plantation in Mississippi, he was in almost every facet of his life related to the traditional southern landed elite. Although his public life was divided between politics and the practice of law, from his earliest days until the end of his life, he remained a cotton planter.

A short, untidy man with shaggy hair and unkempt mustache, Williams was an extremely gregarious creature whose convivial qualities were sometimes punctuated with a sharp wit usually leveled at pomposity or hypocrisy. He thought of

was opposed personally, for the Federal Trade Commission Act. He also supported all four of those awesomely precedent-setting federal subsidies to the states, incorporated in the Smith-Hughes Act, the first direct grants to secondary schools on a national basis, the Smith-Lever Agricultural Extension Act, Farm Loan's Act, and the Federal Highways Act.

In 1928 when Williams was backing Alfred E. Smith, he wrote he would support even a Jew for President "if he were a good Democratic Jew." In much the same spirit Williams voted for Wilson's appointment of Louis D. Brandeis to the Supreme Court, when many of his southern colleagues were opposed. Thus one is never sure whether Williams in backing an administration measure was voting his convictions, registering his devotion to the Democratic Party as it then was, or exhibiting his intense loyalty to Woodrow Wilson. A better index of his own personal convictions therefore may lay in his points of opposition to Wilson's sponsored program.

Williams opposed the President on immigration restriction, women's suffrage, and child labor regulation. Although he and other southern members of Congress were to couch their public opposition to proposals in terms of their fear of the augmentation of federal power, their position on the remainder of Wilson's program strongly suggests that most of their votes were really animated by racial and class feelings. Thus Williams was for immigration restrictions because of the "indigestible inferior peoples" then swarming into the country. He would support women's suffrage, he wrote, if it were limited to white women. And his opposition to child labor, one can infer, was related to the planters' need for the cheapest of all labor, white or black.

The white supremacists of the South had little to complain of in Wilson's more direct handling of the racial question. During his eight-year term the position of the Negro in the federal government deteriorated markedly from what it had been under the two previous Republican administrations. Consequently, there was little need for southerners to wash their racial linen in public except on the local and state level. But the intensity of Williams' racial convictions is a matter of record. In 1904 he remarked that the one thing he loved beyond all things including his wife and the Democratic Party was "the purity and the integrity and the supremacy of white races everywhere." The Mississippian was convinced that the existing supremacy of the whites was biologically determined. If the blacks were at some time in the future given a college education, he argued, their relative position as against that of the whites would remain the same, since the latter would have advanced just as much, if not more. Williams, however, was not content to leave the result to genetics entirely. He hedged his bet by proposing outright discrimination in educational opportunities. In his 1907–1908 campaign for the Senate against James K. Vardaman, the contest was characterized by Vardaman's boast that as governor, while dramatically improving white schools he had denied an increase to Negro institutions. Williams answered that he was vehemently opposed to technical education for the black race because it would bring the Negro "into competition with white mechanics and artisans."

Just as dangerous as the black threat to Williams' beloved Black Belt feudal society was that of the poor whites, especially if it were crystalized in an organized political or economic form distinct from the Democratic Party. His opposition to the Populists had been based upon an intense feeling that the state should be represented by the cultivated and the able; but his continuing success as a politician depended on the support of many of the poorer whites of the state. Consequently, he would never go on record, as his friends and neighbors the Percys did, that the poor white breed was below contempt and, overall, inferior to the Negro. Concealing his class feelings he therefore hid his opposition to Vardaman, the champion of the poor white of the state, swallowed his opinions on the labor provision of the Clayton Act, and argued his case against the child labor amendment on the grounds of federal power and states' rights. World War I and its aftermath, however, triggered his pro-British upper-class feelings against peace advocates, the rising Negro expectations, and the vigorous challenge of organized labor. Williams wanted to expel his colleague Vardaman along with Robert La Follette from the Senate because of their peace stands, called the West Virginia coal strike in 1919 "a conspiracy to commit murder," and demanded that all national strikes such as the steel and the railroad work stoppages be arbitrated by a federal board on which so-called "public members" would hold the balance of power. Any group opposed to public arbitration, he stated, with specific reference to the unions, was "seeking some selfish and illegitimate purpose." And though Williams had proudly stated on the floor of the Senate in 1918 that he did not belong "to the nigger-hating and nigger-baiting class of the South," when the Republican majority proposed an antilynching bill in 1921, this urbane, kindly, and usually tolerant man ended his Senatorial career with an emotional defense of lynching.

Probably John Sharp Williams never consciously related his passionate stand on the race and organized labor questions or his attitude toward the blacks and the poor whites in so many words. But the relationship obviously existed as did their mutual challenge to his beloved class-ridden society of the Mississippi Delta, to which in 1922 he voluntarily retired probably as much disgusted with himself as with the times.

Among the more important trends in American politics during the twenties and early thirties was the gradual urbanization of the national Democratic Party. The conservative tone of the Republicans alienated many union officials and social workers and their clients in the rapidly growing cities. Alfred E. Smith's 1928 Presidential campaign, building upon a historic Irish base, attracted to the Democrats many urban Catholics. But perhaps the mass movement of the northern urban Negro into the Democratic ranks was the most startling development. More than three million southern Negroes had moved North between 1910 and 1930, and they were soon followed by a flood of black people during the depression, pushed by the decline of southern cotton culture and attracted by the more nearly color-blind and usually more generous relief programs in the northern cities. Consequently, hitherto safe Republican states like New York, Massachusetts, Connecticut, Rhode Island, New Jersey, Michigan, and Illinois were safe no longer. As the power of the urban Democratic organizations grew, that of the other traditional power base of the party—the Democratic South—decreased.

44

The shifting balance of power in the 1933–37 Democratic Party is perhaps seen most clearly by contrasting the regional complexion of Franklin Roosevelt's important advisers with those of the Wilson administration. Only three of Roosevelt's cabinet were southerners, and of these, only Cordell Hull could be said to be influential. Of just a shade less importance in policy roles were Roosevelt's White House assistants and advisers. Collectively called the Brain Trust, they included Rexford G. Tugwell, Adolph A. Berle, Jr., and Raymond Moley, and later Donald Richberg, Thomas G. Corcoran, Benjamin Cohen, Felix Frankfurter, and a galaxy of lesser stars. None of these men were southerners, most were nonpoliticians, and practically all were from the urbanized Northeast. Early in the administration the leaders of Capitol Hill and the new group about the President recognized each other as rivals and often as potential enemies.

But if the South had lost some of its power, that fact could not be ascertained from the makeup of the Congressional establishment. For a short time after March 4, 1933, Henry T. Rainey of Illinois was Speaker of the House. But at his death Joseph W. Byrns of Tennessee inherited the position to be followed in the Roosevelt years by William B. Bankhead of Alabama and Sam Rayburn of Texas. In the extraordinary session of 1933, twelve of the seventeen major House committees were chaired by southerners. During Roosevelt's first two terms the Senate was presided over by John Nance Garner of Texas. Until his death in 1937, Joseph T. Robinson was majority floor leader. The President's other important advisers were James F. Byrnes of South Carolina and Pat Harrison of Mississippi. Nine of the fourteen chairmen of major Senate committees were also from the South.

Most of these powerful southerners were self-labeled conservatives, and not a few were called reactionaries by other people. But a majority of them had supported Franklin Roosevelt's nomination, and most of them, the two Virginia senators being the great exceptions, consistently voted for the major New Deal measures until the Court plan of 1937. Even then two-thirds of the southern senators announced their support for Court reform. Such strong support was also true of the House. For example, North Carolina's Robert Doughton, Chairman of the House Ways and Means Committee, a mountain farmer and a mule trader, cast his first vote against a major administration proposal in 1941. Rarely in all political history has a group of so-called conservatives and reactionaries so consistently voted for radical and reform measures over as long a period of years as did these southerners. The startling fact

46

needs explanation, and perhaps some understanding of the paradox can be gained by looking at one of the most conservative of the southern Democratic senators, Josiah W. Bailey of North Carolina.

Perhaps as well as any man Senator Bailey typifies the tension between the southern Senator as a conservative and as a New Deal supporter. Born of a Baptist, middle-class clerical family, he succeeded his father as the editor of a Baptist publication. But he soon entered politics and though he obviously lusted for political office, he was denied an elected position until 1930 when he defeated Senator Furnifold M. Simmons mainly on the charge that the incumbent had betrayed the party by not supporting Alfred E. Smith in 1928. Symptomatic of Bailey's entire career, except on two issues, was the fact that he himself had been opposed to Smith until he heard that Simmons was also opposed. Seven years later, of course, Bailey was a leader in the attempt to create a Republican-Democratic coalition to dump Roosevelt in 1940. In a similar fashion Bailey's early career defies ideological analysis. Although his friendly biographer states that he was a liberal during his younger days, Bailey in reality oscillated between the liberal and conservative camps in North Carolina politics as chance and opportunity offered. A staunch prohibitionist who drank and a fervent oral legalist who broke the state's games laws at will, Bailey as readily changed the color of his political coat as possible preferment appeared.

An angular-featured man of cold and humorless guise, he was of even temperament—usually irritable, at least in public. In Washington he had little influence outside of that commanded by his position, having few close friends either in the administration or among his colleagues. Schlesinger mentions him only twice in his three volumes on the New Deal, and he was known among his Senatorial peers as "Holy Joe." If Bailey's early political acts were extremely flexible in their ideological orientation, his basic economic and social assumptions, at least in his private writing, were largely fixed by 1932. He maintained he owed most of his ideas to Edmund Burke, Adam Smith, and John Adams. Although he rarely quoted any of that venerable triad, he did object to Roosevelt's campaign statement that economic laws were man-made, arguing that the acceptable doctrine of the last 150 years had asserted that "fundamental economic laws are natural laws, having the same force as physical laws. . . ." Except for that exerted by North Carolina financial & industrial interests and selected out of state corporations, Bailey was a foe of what he called "concentrated power." He was also extremely fearful of the masses, writing after the 1936 campaign that the trouble with democracy was that "after it gets free to do what it pleases, it usually does the wrong thing." Bailey was also an inveterate budget balancer and antilabor union man. His biographer, however, denies this stating that he approved of unions; he was opposed only to strikes.

Against such an ideological background Bailey's record in Roosevelt's first term is highly interesting. During the hundred days he voted against the Beer and Wine act and expressed opposition to the granting of direct federal relief and the price fixing features of the Agriculture Adjustment Administration but voted affirmatively on the final roll call of relief and agricultural measures. He also voted for twenty-odd other major bills including the Tennessee Valley Authority, the Securities and Exchange Act, National Industrial Recovery Act, and Farm Credit acts. During 1934 he contented himself by supporting amendments to scale down relief acts and then voting for the final acts.

In the face of repeated polls showing huge popular support for the New Deal in North Carolina as well as throughout the South, Bailey, facing a re-election in 1936, moderated both his public rhetoric and his meager negative voting habits. In 1935 and 1936 he did manage to cast votes against the National Labor Relations Act and the Guffey Coal Act. But he supported the Social Security Act, the "soak the rich" taxation proposal, and the Walsh-Healey Act providing for minimum wages and maximum hours on government contract work. On most other controversial legislation, including banking and the public utility holding company acts, he refused to vote, writing to a friend that it "was much wiser to keep one's thoughts to himself."

During the 1936 campaign, it was difficult at times to tell whether Bailey was campaigning for himself, for Roosevelt, or for the entire New Deal. But even when wearing Roosevelt's protective mantle and running against a weak opponent, the senator's primary victory was not impressive. In November the President out-polled the senator by over 200,000 votes. Nevertheless, Bailey commented that he considered the election a conservative victory and that he was returning to Washington as a "conservative." The following year he was adamant against the reform of the Supreme Court and was one of the leaders in the unsuccessful attempt to form a Democratic-Republican conservative coalition. From that time on Bailey was almost invariably opposed to New Deal measures except when they aided the growers of tobacco, cotton, and peanuts. His record on tax measures, for example, is fairly indicative of his general voting habits. In 1938 he supported both the repeal of the undistributed profits tax and the lowering of capital gains measures. During the war period he was against raising the surtaxes on personal income and for larger capital gains exemptions. And even though North Carolina was virtually without deposits of oil, copper, and coal, he voted for increased depletion allowances.

In addition to the senator's basic conservatism and his inclination to do what he felt he had to do in order to remain in office, two other threads of consistency run through his record, namely his attitudes toward labor and race. Aside from the Supreme Court fight, it is obvious from his correspondence that no other issues raised his spleen as did the actions of unions or the threat of national intervention in the existing racial patterns.

Senator Bailey did vote for the NIRA with its famous section 7a and for the Walsh-Healey government contracts act. But the first measure promised aid to, and was supported by, the textile industry, and the second moved through Congress just before his election campaign of 1936. Otherwise Bailey's record is consistently and emotionally an antilabor one, the intensity of his feeling appearing during the war years. In 1941 he demanded that work stoppages be defined as "sabotage." A year later he called the nation's labor leaders "tyrants" and in 1944 he supported the Brewster "work or fight" bill which proposed to draft all men up to age forty-five not working in essential war industries and place them in such at service pay. Two years later he approved Truman's proposal to induct striking railroad and coal workers into the army. Such actions could have been inspired by patriotism, but in view of the senator's wartime record on profits, income surtaxes, and capital gains, they were also obviously animated by a deep prejudice for capital and against labor.

Bailey's opposition to modifying the racial status quo was just as consistent as his position on labor. In 1933 he threatened, apropos of the Wagner anti-lynching bill, that the South would not tolerate a Democratic Party seeking Negro votes. A year later he joined the filibuster against a similar bill. Since FDR's public record on Negro rights was extremely ambiguous, Bailey spared the President any racial criticism until 1937. But after the overturning of the two-thirds rule in the 1936 convention, he was increasingly convinced that Roosevelt and his northern labor allies had a well-thought-out plan to change the nature of the national Democratic Party. The Court reform bill, the creation of federal jobs by the thousands in the big cities, and outright relief were all elements in a scheme first to get northern Negro support and then ultimately to face the South with "a new Reconstruction Era." After 1937 he repeatedly referred to the national Democratic

Party as one dominated by city bosses, blacks, and labor barons.

For the New Deal era it is certainly questionable whether one can properly call James F. Byrnes a conservative. He has been described variously for the period as an ally of the "conservative Bourbon businessmen" of his state, as a "protector of the northern imperial interest," a "liberal, not of a radical or conservative predilection," and as a "New Dealer." In his autobiography Byrnes refers to himself as a "conservative liberal, trying to restrain the extremists of the right and left," which would seem to put him in the Eisenhower category. But if one looks at his total career, as a protégé of Senator Benjamin R. (Pitchfork Ben) Tillman, as a young congressman, as a senator during the latter days of the prewar New Deal, and subsequently as an ardent foe of Truman's Fair Deal, and finally as governor of Southern Carolina, he could, one would estimate, be called a conservative, although a remarkably deviant one from the usual southern pattern.

Byrnes was born in Charleston of a working-class father and mother. He quit school at the age of fourteen to work in a law office and to help his widowed mother who faced the problem of raising a family. Thereafter his natural attractiveness, obvious intelligence, and remarkable industry, plus his almost uncanny lifelong ability to make friends among the powerful, propelled him forward to the state bar, to the office of prosecuting attorney, and finally at the age of twenty-nine by the grace of fifty-seven votes, to Congress. Long before that event, Byrnes had been adopted by the ruling South Carolina oligarchy. He was relected eleven times to the House from Senator Tillman's home district before losing a race for the Senate in 1924 to Coleman Blease. But after a six-year interim of representing large corporations in Spartanburg and at Washington, he defeated Blease in 1930.

Few men have risen faster in the United States Senate than Byrnes. Befriended by practically all of the party establishment and aided by his early support of and friendship with Franklin Roosevelt, he was appointed to the powerful Appropriations Committee and soon became, along with Robinson of Arkansas and Harrison of Mississippi, an administration leader. Even after 1937 when he had become an opponent of most of the New Deal's domestic economic policies, he remained the President's trusted representative to Congress for foreign affairs. After America's entrance into World War II, Byrnes became, in Roosevelt's words, the "Assistant President," and virtually the dictator of war mobilization, and hence, of domestic affairs. In

1940 and again in 1944 he unquestionably would have been nominated Vice President and thus would have succeeded to the Presidency in 1945 had it not been for Roosevelt's capitulation to the big northern city bosses and the leaders of organized labor. As a sop for his disappointments he was appointed by Roosevelt to the Supreme Court where he was not particularly happy. Later he served as Truman's Secretary of State.

A charming and graceful gentleman, Byrnes's legislative and administrative genius lay in his ability to find a viable compromise between contending factions. He rarely made speeches on the floor of the Senate, but his work in committees found paths through legislative thickets and saved Roosevelt from many a defeat at the hands of Congress. He was disinclined to engage in public controversy, refused to deal in personalities, and yet could be decisive as his record as war administrator indicates. Byrnes was one of the most attractive and able men in the public life of his times, and measured by achievements, he was certainly the most influential southern member of Congress between John Calhoun and Lyndon Johnson.

Except on Wilson's defense and foreign policy, Byrnes's record is a remarkably consistent one, from his earliest days in Congress until the spring of 1937. His vote was recorded for almost every one of the New Freedom's major reforms, including women's suffrage. And save for his opposition to the "death sentence clause" for utility holding companies, he continued to support liberal and even radical proposals through the first four years of the New Deal. Among his most significant affirmative votes were those for the Wagner labor act, for which he won an American Federation of Labor endorsement in 1936, and the "soak the rich" tax bill.

The senator's loyalty even weathered the 1937 Supreme Court struggle. But the New Deal's continued support of heavy relief expenditures in the northern cities and its continued prolabor stance at a time when the Committee for Industrial Organization was organizing unskilled labor in industrial unions and when sitdown strikes were inflaming the capital-labor issue, ignited his opposition to Roosevelt's domestic program. Like many southern members of Congress and middle westerners, for that matter, Byrnes grew increasingly apprehensive of the rising power of both the big city bosses and of organized labor in the Democratic Party. From the spring of 1937 on, he sought to reduce relief appropriations and to introduce more local control of all public funds. In 1937 he voted against the national housing bill and introduced an amendment to the Guffey coal bill to outlaw sitdown strikes. During

the following year he discreetly aided the targets of
Roosevelt's purge, supported a reduction in the capital gains tax as well as an increase in the depletion
allowances for extractive industries. Subsequently
he demanded a southern differential in wages paid
under the proposed wage and hour act, participated
as a Supreme Court justice in findings which organized labor considered antiunion, and insisted as the
wartime director of civilian mobilization, over labor's objection, on a "hold the line" position with
reference to wages and prices.

In public Byrnes argued against continued heavy
relief appropriations. Because of the huge unemployment in the northern cities and the higher wages
in the North, he stated the South and his own state
were being shortchanged. That was a startling
charge since South Carolina and the entire South
received from the federal treasury far more dollars
per capita and per dollar paid in income taxes than
any other section of the country. And as a budget
and appropriation expert, Byrnes certainly must
have been aware of the existing true ratios. What
more probably troubled the South Carolinian was
the shifting balance within the Democratic Party
and its implications for southern racial and wage
policies. In a private letter Byrnes admitted as much
by pointing out that 80 percent of Washington

D.C.'s relief payments was made to Negroes and that elsewhere in the country the power of the city and labor bosses went up with every increase in relief appropriations.

Byrnes was no public race baiter, refusing many times to debate the problem even in hard fought election campaigns. But throughout his career his position against changing the then existing basis of racial relations in the South is remarkably consistent. As a young congressman he was against appropriations to Howard University, opposed the 1917 draft in part because it did not specifically provide for segregation in the forces, and questioned Wilson's child labor proposals as a possible entering wedge for federal intervention into the race problem. During the postwar hysteria over radicalism, race riots, and militant labor, Byrnes made two impassioned statements on race. His often quoted remarks defending lynching and imputing the inequality of the races to God were never again to be repeated by him from a public rostrum. But they lifted the curtain for a moment on the raw inner passion that continued to dominate a corner of the mentality of this unusually rational and tolerant man.

Byrnes's surprising decision in 1950 to forsake retirement and run for the governorship of South Carolina was obviously tied to his intense opposition to particular parts of Harry Truman's Fair Deal. During his campaign he attacked many items of the Truman program including those devoted to "federally regimented" agriculture, business, and medicine. Since he had in the past supported many such measures of similar social purport, his philosophic objections to the Brannan plan could not have cut too deeply. Rather, his more intense objections were centered upon the northern bossism and the socialism that characterized this "new Democratic Party." What he meant precisely by that term was made clear in a February 6, 1952, speech given to the Georgia Assembly. The Democratic National Convention of 1948, he asserted, had been controlled by a labor-Negro coalition which had constituted the "balance of power" in at least eleven very large states, and as a consequence the party had "abandoned its traditional principles and adopted a platform more socialistic than Democratic." As governor of South Carolina his more positive prescription was the maintenance of segregated education and a right to work law. And although Governor Byrnes did secure from a reluctant legislature the appropriation of millions for the education of blacks, his program in essence meant continuing the relative positions in the state of the three large social classes, the existing elite, the poor white, and the Negro. Byrnes's support of Eisenhower in 1952, Harry F.

# III

## The Persistent Elite

The preceding chapter examined three southern Democratic Senatorial conservatives of diverse social and geographical origins whose collective careers spanned the first half of the twentieth century. Privately all three exhibited the stock southern conservative responses of their day—a fear of direct democracy and the growth of federal power, support for states' rights and a balanced budget, a benign attitude toward the wealthier elite in the nation, a particular concern for the landed man, and a marked suspicion of large cities and particularly of the political organization of their lower economic classes.

The public voting records of these three southern conservatives, when cast against their philosophical predilections, seemingly constitute one of the most glaring paradoxes in American political history. For over the fifty years their votes and those of their fellow southern senators became a powerful factor in the creation of the modern centralized social service state whose constantly expanding federal bureacracy and correlated federal power almost denied the reality of their alleged cherished convictions. Without the support of the southern conservatives in committees and on record votes, the New Freedom and New Deal reforms would have been greatly altered, possibly beyond recognition, a fact which Woodrow Wilson and Franklin Roosevelt constantly kept in mind.

This strange career of southern conservatism is even more paradoxical when it is further cast against that of the western middle western conservatives. For if my thesis in the first chapter has any validity, then very similar societies in both sections should have produced like political responses, as they did, for example, during the Populist period. But a glance at the total voting record of the western middle western senators during the New Freedom and New Deal days indicates that by any objective political rating, the western agrarians would fall much further toward the conservative end of the spectrum than that occupied by their southern colleagues of allegedly similar persuasion. When viewed from existing historical accounts this is rather strange since the Middle West has been traditionally pictured as one of the seedbeds of progressivism in an earlier period and as being the locale of heavy New Deal Democratic gains.

During the Wilson period the western middle western senators as a group, of course, supported the New Freedom's proagricultural legislation. But on other major items of Wilson's program their voting was anything but consistently for the so-called liberal measures which were almost unanimously supported by the southern conservatives. Thus seven votes from the section were either cast or paired against the Clayton amendment to the Sherman Anti-Trust Act, two against the Federal Trade Commission, five against the federal highways bill of 1916, three might be interpreted as against the Smith-Hughes vocational education bill, although no formal vote was recorded, and even three against the Smith-Lever agricultural extension enactment. Small wonder that a southern conservative remarked that the group refused either to lead or to be led toward progressive legislation. The differential in voting records continued during the New Deal period. Whereas the southern conservatives, Glass and Byrd of Virginia to the exception, supported Roosevelt's major legislative requests until 1937–38, eleven of the fourteen western middle western senators opposed the labor provisions of the

National Recovery Administration, five were against the Walsh-Healey Act, and six of eight voted "no" on the Fair Labor Standards Act of July, 1937. Slightly smaller negative totals were registered against increasing relief appropriations and on the "soak the rich" taxation bill of 1935. By comparison with western middle western counterparts the southern conservatives appeared by any index of voting to be staunchly liberal or progressive.

Some of the more romantic historians have explained this southern conservative aberration in terms of loyalty to the Democratic Party. Unquestionably southern history and historic emotional attachments played some part in their actions. But the impressive departures from the party during the Populist period and the wholesale desertion after 1946 indicates that traditions in politics not supported by bread and butter issues are soon eroded.

A look at the record will indicate that the southern conservatives had a good many nonromantic reasons for their ties to what was an essentially progressive or a liberal national party. Basic to most of these reasons was the rock-bottom fact that throughout the first fifty years of the century and indeed up to the present, under Democratic and Republican presidents, they steadily held one of the two main centers of power in the party, the Congressional committee structure, and thus except in extraordinary times and on extraordinary issues the Congressional power to pass or defeat a legislative program. By their own ability to return to Congress, no matter what the outcome of the national canvass, by their own natural longevity, by the powerful committee system ruled by seignority and by the interesting phenomenon that liberal Democrats do not hold office as long in the South as conservatives —Lyndon Johnson and Albert A. Gore are two of the few liberal long-livers who come to mind—the southern conservative virtually made the Congressional party his own. By virtue of the workings of its committee system Congress has often been described as an oligarchic body or more lately as a gerontocracy. On the Democratic side of the aisle it might be just as well dubbed a *southernocracy*. James MacGregor Burns's discovery of a four-party system during the 1960's—two centered on the White House and two on Capitol Hill—has been true of the Democratic Party at least since 1900. The power, the glory, and the spoils coming from this situation have been considerable.

Even before the New Deal the perquisites of a committee chairman in either house were handsome. And during later years the power of a chairman to allocate pork to his own district or state has advanced almost geometrically. As a young member of the House Appropriations Committee, James F.

Byrnes was satisfied that a few federal grants for his district's roads were enough to keep the natives satisfied. But as a member of the similar Senate committee during the New Deal, he obviously felt it was necessary to spend a good deal of effort wringing the multi-billion-dollar Santee River project from a reluctant Secretary of Interior, Harold Ickes, whose belief that the proposal was a huge waste of money has since been proved correct. Other instances of the spectacular milking of the public purse for parochial purposes are not hard to find. When the New Deal Senate majority leader Joseph Robinson complained that he was in a hellish agony of spirit because he was personally against a New Deal measure and yet due to his position had to support it, a colleague sourly observed that Robinson's personal road to perdition had been paved with an astronomical number of new Arkansas post offices. And Senator Pat Harrison's boast, while running for reelection in 1936, that Mississippi had received more per capita federal funds than any other state in the Union, is eloquent of the southern uses of pork at its most utilitarian level.

Economists and historians are agreed that the South received more from the New Deal in total federal subsidies as measured against payment in taxes than any other section in the nation. And the annual figures of the sixties indicating that the re-

World War II Europe between the democratic West and the communist East. Neither side of the bargainers, whether Russia or the West or the North or the South, could afford to affirm publicly that such an agreement existed. Understandably factions and individuals on either side occasionally acted as if nothing prevented their taking a free hand in matters normally reserved for the other. And yet powerful politicians of both North and South were sensitive or were made sensitive to its demands. New liberal and northern Democratic Presidents were especially made aware of the costs of transgression. Wilson started his administration by attempting to appoint Democratic Negroes for Republican ones until he was sharply reminded by southern Congressional leaders that his actions would cost him votes in support of his legislative program. And though Roosevelt was personally in sympathy with the 1934 Wagner antilynching proposal he replied to its northern advocates, who wanted him to make the bill an administration measure, that its time had not yet come. Its time never came during the New Deal years even during the war when patriotism and the rhetoric of the four freedoms might have eased its passage. The effect of the black-inspired wartime creation of the Fair Employment Practices Committee was largely negated by southern opposition and a most politically minded President. When faced directly by the refusal of the southern railroads to abide by a committee order, Roosevelt dodged a decision by referring the dispute to a mediation committee, which in the course of three years could never come to an acceptable finding. The FEPC came to the end of its road in June, 1946, by want of Congressional appropriations.

Meanwhile in 1938 another antilynching proposal had created a crisis in the party by reason of the fact that fifty-five northern Congressional Democrats had endorsed the measure. Excited by this *démarche* of historically dependable allies, Senator Byrnes of South Carolina took the Senate floor to recite some history, comment on the changing nature of the Democratic Party, and offer a prophecy about its troubled future. A similar bill, he recalled, had been initiated by the House Republican majority in 1921. But then twenty northern Democrats had supported their southern colleagues in defeating it. Now it was being sponsored by a northern Democrat with the support of fifty-four of his kind. If the measure came to a vote in the Senate, Byrnes was sure it would be passed by Democratic vote. That constituted a revolutionary change in the party brought about because "90 percent of the Negroes in the North . . . are voting for Democratic candidates. The Negro has not only come into the Democratic Party," the senator added, "the Negro has come into *control* of the Democratic Party." Consequently the South would have to reappraise its political attachments, the senator hinted. For although the section "had never voted for a Republican candidate," it was obvious that "the white people in the South in supporting the Democratic Party has been due to the belief that when problems affecting the Negro and the very soul of the South arose, they could depend upon the Democrats of the North to rally to their support. . . ."

Byrnes's thrust was obviously made to be heard in the White House as well as in the North. During the following filibuster, even though Roosevelt had not initiated the measure, the Senator told the President's son that the bill would be on the floor and thus tie up other wanted legislation for a hundred years unless the President withdrew it. Twice the northern Democrats attempted to end the filibuster by attempting closure, and twice they were defeated by a combination of southern Democrats and Republicans. Since only one Republican senator voted to end debate, the historic roles of the two northern parties on the race question were reversed, facilitating the Republican-Democratic coalition during the late Truman years and the Eisenhower administrations.

Byrnes's speech with its threat to leave the Democrats and join the Republicans was, of course, the first twentieth-century expression of today's so-called southern strategy, differing from the latter formula only in that it was initiated by a southern Democrat seeking Republican support for the southern solution of the race question rather than by a Republican Presidential candidate seeking southern votes for victory.

Byrnes's passionate relating of the "soul of the South" with the maintenance of black subordination, by the terror of lynching if necessary, is also eloquent testimony to the fact that the existing racial pattern was basic to the mentality of the southern political conservative and his business and professional supporters. The twin facts that an almost concurrent poll had indicated a slight southern popular majority in favor of an antilynching statute and that Byrnes did leave his party over the question fourteen years later give further point to the observation. States' rights, home rule, laissez faire, the Democratic Party, all might be bargained away as many of these issues had been in the past. But race was the *sine qua non* of his political demands, the very "soul" of his particular South. That it should be advanced on the floor of the Senate in such emotional and dogmatic terms by Jimmy Byrnes is revelatory of the intensity with which the issue was held by himself and by his clientele. Byrnes was a lifelong moderate, a conciliator between the conflicting views advanced by a much fragmented party. For years he had been the respected broker between the White House and Congress. He had rarely been a public race baiter, and since he had just been re-elected, he stood in no immediate need of popular support. All the available evidence would seem to indicate that his racial views in the intense 1938 debate were his own and those of his closest associates and friends, which by this stage in his life happened to be clustered among the powerful politicians and the propertied establishment of his state. Collectively this multifaceted establishment might be described as, for the want of a better term, the southern power elite.

One of the neglected areas of recent southern history is this southern elite and its relationship to the area's politicians. Of the latter, of course, scores of political studies exist, and Cash's *Mind of the South* and similar works have explored the mentality of the region's articulate writers, professors, and editors. But relatively little has been done with the class or classes that owned most of the area's resources, the manufacturers, merchants, bankers, landowners, and their related professionals. In commenting upon this group, even such an expert in southern decision making as V. O. Key, Jr., had to use an equivocal phrase: "The South," he stated, *"may* have a relatively small economic elite that possesses high cohesion amid the corollary power of discipline of dissenters." Key was more certain, however, of the social results of the elite's actions. "The outcome," he records, has been "a social and economic structure in which the gulf between the rich and the poor has been extraordinarily wide." Whatever the origins of this economic disparity, and probably many of them lay deep in the section's history, during the twentieth century no other large agricultural area in the nation produced the massive differentials in income that existed between the southern elite, the yeoman farmers, and the mass of the poor whites and the Negro population on the bottom of the economic heap. On the basis of present evidence the main thrust of the southern conservative politicians and their commercial and professional allies has been to maintain this disparity, to see that the proper people were in their proper place on top, the masses of the poorer whites were near the bottom, and the Negro held in virtual poverty. The record of their success is written in beating back the twin threats of liberal or progressive state governments and of labor unions, in maintaining the wage differentials between classes within the South, and by comparison to those existing elsewhere in the nation, and in holding to a minimum federal intervention in either the industrial or the race question. For, as I hope to show, the racial issue was inextricably intertwined with the others, acting as a vital and basic instrument in securing most of the other social objectives, and in the last analysis probably was a talisman of reassurance, that despite southern reformers and Yankee meddlers, the conscience of intellectuals and preachers, things were much as they had been, and southern society secure.

Following the political and social disfranchisement of the Negro and the defeat of the Populists, the main challenge to the southern elite came from the continued political organization of the poorer white classes residing mainly on the land. Few more bitter political campaigns have been fought in the nation than those between the partisans of the James K. Vardaman-Theodore G. Bilbo tradition in Mississippi, the Tom Watson-Hoke Smith followers in Georgia, those of the early Longs of Louisiana, and the usually more refined and educated representatives of the upper social classes. Where and when successful, these southern agrarians or progressive administrations secured real if limited gains for their supporters as Dewey Grantham and George Tindall have shown. The incidence of taxation was shifted marginally, railroads—and in time other utilities—were regulated, hard-surfaced

roads were built into the countryside, public medicine and charitable institutions were improved, and
most important over the long term, public education
for the poor whites was extended and better fi-
nanced.

The white challenge most meaningful for the future in reordering the southern classes, however,
probably came from the infant labor unions. In the
years immediately after World War I the section
for the first time became widely preoccupied with
the local problem of organized labor. And though
the average southern millhand had probably never
heard of Bakunin or Marx, his organizations were
ascribed to both, and his activities were called "that
unholy, foreign-born, un-American, despotic thing
*known* as *labor unionism.*" Simultaneous national
strikes which penetrated the South in the coal and
steel industries prompted Senator John Sharp Williams' remark that organized labor's activities were
a "conspiracy to commit murder." A nationwide
propaganda pro-American antiunion campaign, the
short but sharp postwar depression, and the organized power of the southern commonwealths from the
governor down to the sheriff and local constabulary
broke the strikes and destroyed the unions as they
did in many other parts of the country. By 1921,
except in a very few skilled occupations, unions had
disappeared, and southern employers could exult in

saving the American way, exclaiming once again, as one South Carolina mill manager had before the trouble: "We govern like the Czar of Russia."

However thinly, the dragon's teeth of unionism had been sown in the southern poor white consciousness. The dread spectre of the organized poor whites emerged again in the troubled textile industry and again in the coal and iron industries. From 1928–29 until World War II the armed forces of the southern states were mobilized to a maximum degree more often against white unionism than against the somnolent blacks. Gastonia, North Carolina, and Harlan County, Kentucky, before the election of Roosevelt, and a hundred other places afterward, contributed paragraphs to the history of violence between organized labor and the more potent organized state.

Under the more benign social climate of the early New Deal when the most critical nationwide decisions involving labor and capital were transferred from the state capitals to Washington, the flickering and uncertain life of southern white unionism was resuscitated, often with the reluctant help of southern conservative senators, coerced perhaps as much by their awareness of the intense New Deal inclinations of their constituents as by the already mentioned elusive but demonstrable bargain with the northern Democratic Party.

At the minimum under the New Deal labor legislation, skilled-craft unions gained a toehold, especially in the rapidly growing urban regions of the South from which it was impossible to remove them. And gradually under the aegis of the Wagner labor act industrial unions slowly took root. Admittedly the economic condition of southern poor white labor, whether on the land or in the shop, was ameliorated by the impact of relief and reform legislation, although the effects of the New Deal's agricultural program on the small and tenant farmers was at best a mixed bag of debits and credits. Moreover, when all the economic blessings showered on the region are carefully counted, those filtering down to the laboring classes are often more apparent than real. This was largely due to already existing wage patterns, to the repeated inclusion of clauses in many of New Deal acts permitting regional differentials, to the local administration, or maladministration of many national reforms, to subsequent state legislative action, and finally to the existence in the region of a second and even more depressed laboring class, the Negro.

The force of the existing standards on wages is perhaps best illustrated by the facts that Franklin Roosevelt paid his farm laborers at Warm Springs the sum of twenty dollars per month, whereas the equivalent figure for Kansas was 50 percent more.

Since the pay for relief work was often tied to existing local standards, WPA wages in the South often amounted to about 50 percent of those paid in the North. Latitude for regional differentials was written into the NRA act, and as a consequence the Textile Code permitted a national minimum wage of thirteen dollars per week except for the South where it was twelve dollars. State variances were, of course, permitted in the Social Security Act, and the retirement provision containing a very low national minimum was mainly calculated on the basis of an individual's previous earning pattern. Constrained by the evident popularity of a minimum wage and hour enactment—both the spring primaries and a series of Gallup polls had so attested—most southern conservative senators voted for the 1938 Black-Connery Fair Labor Standards Act, which set a national pay minimum of forty cents per hour and a maximum of forty hours of labor per week. But the Act, while establishing the important principle of a national floor, was so riddled with exemptions and qualifications that its actual immediate results fell far below the expectations of its supporters.

The wage and hour bill was the last significant New Deal labor victory. Thereafter southern conservative senators contributed significantly to the rapidly ebbing labor reform tide. According to Professor Key, the majority of southern senators from 1933 until 1945 voted against the administration more often on labor legislation than on every other type of issue. After that date their antilabor record was even more consistent. Only two southern votes were cast against the 1946 Case bill banning strikes for sixty days and outlawing the secondary boycott. The following year only four southern Senatorial votes were cast against the overriding of Truman's veto of the Taft-Hartley Act. And as late as 1958, only six southern votes supported Senator John Kennedy's measure to extend unemployment compensation to sixteen weeks.

During the debate over the wage and hour legislation Senator "Cotton Ed" Smith defended his vehement opposition to the measure as based upon the right to maintain "the splendid gifts of God to the South," one of which, the senator explained elsewhere was the ability of any worker to live in South Carolina on fifty cents per day. Subsequently southern legislators have sought to give more positive aid to the deity by guaranteeing the right to work without belonging or paying dues to a union. By the end of the 1950's every southern state except Kentucky had some variety of a right to work law upon its statute books. In addition to the unions, the maintenance of a differential wage between the races has also concerned the southern elite.

Variance between wages of the blacks and whites was often justified or perhaps rationalized on the basis of the different levels of skills and the rates of productivity exhibited by the two races. At other times the existing differential rates have simply been postulated and accepted as something akin to the laws of the Persians and the Medes. "You cannot prescribe the same wages for the black man as for the white man," representative Martin Dies of Texas exclaimed. But whatever justification has been made for differential wages between the races, there is little doubt that the low wage rate for blacks has at least marginally affected that of the lowest paid whites. There seems to be a law of very rough correspondence in wages even in a not so free labor market, with the scales ascending imperfectly in relation to supply, relative class power, skills, and society's overall judgment as to the inherent or more often mythical value, the necessity or usefulness of the labor performed. Consequently, the continued existence of a large pool of extremely low regarded, low paid black labor in the South has probably skewered the entire wage scale of the section downward. In other words, low paid black labor has, to a degree, meant low paid white labor.

There was another important employer advantage accrued from the existence of two separate laboring pools in the South. The situation afforded the opportunity to play one race against the other, and by sustaining racial passions, drain off some of the emotions which might have fueled a labor revolt. In the 1924 South Carolina Senatorial contest the loser, James F. Byrnes, could not understand why so many of the state's cotton mill operators should have supported a rabble-rouser like the victor, Coleman L. Blease. Blease was certainly a rabble-rouser, one owner explained to Byrnes, "but all he ever gets the hands excited about is liquor and niggers. Well, we'll drink the liquor and take care of the niggers. Coley will keep the hands quiet." During the same year that the above remark was made about Senator Blease, *The Manufacturers' Record* editorialized upon the relationship between the section's peculiar political institutions and the threat of unionism: "The Solid South," the editorial stated, "means security for every manufacturer trembling under the whiplash of the anarchistic labor leaders." While a precise racial inference from the two preceding quotes was made none too clear in either publication, a logical conclusion from the remarks seems to postulate the following: sustained racial passions meant one-party government, one-party government meant upper-class control, and hence antiunion government, Q.E.D.: a certain level of racial animosity worked to the benefit of the owning classes.

If the general conclusions of the last few paragraphs are sound, then they say volumes about that much heralded and overromanticized topic, the sense of community to be found in the South. That the sense was there, as it is in most rurally oriented societies, no one who knows anything about the region would care to deny. But I would suggest that the loyalties and attachments that did exist were directed not toward one, but to at least three communities, and that the sense of difference and at times antagonism between the three groups was even greater than their mutual bonds of respect and identification.

During the past fifteen years upper-class southerners have had to change radically their long-held estimate that the Negro was deeply and emotionally attached to many traditional southern institutions. Is it possible that they have made the same mistake, and for some of the same reasons, about the emotions of the poorer white classes? Certainly, on the record, the upper-class southerner had little respect for and attachment to his racial kinsman living on the pine barrens, the canebrakes, or the red hills or those working the badly eroded soil or in the mills.

Since the Populist days, whenever the poorer whites organized politically to challenge the ruling establishments throughout the South, they and their leaders were derided with traditional labels of contempt and disdain: woolhats, rednecks, lintheads, peckerwoods. If the thrust was on the industrial front, the well-worn and often grossly inaccurate, but still useful, cries of an imported radicalism were hurled. "I warn John L. Lewis and his Communist cohorts that no second-hand 'carpetbag expedition' in the Southland under the banner of Soviet Russia . . . will be tolerated," Representative Edward Eugene Cox of Georgia expostulated in 1937 when the threat of industrial unionism was at its peak.

Few politicians with a statewide constituency could afford to vent their real thoughts about the majority of the suffrage holders. But many of their business and social associates were less reticent. Writing in 1942, the cultivated William Alexander Percy, scion of a Mississippi Black Belt family, still remembered with rancor the defeat of his father by the Vardaman-led poor whites. He also had the Bilbo machine in Mississippi and the New Deal in Washington very much in mind when he described the mass of whites in his state as the lowest of low, ignorant, lazy, irresponsible, and dishonest, without one redeeming trait of character, and much below the Negro in almost any scale of human virtues. When confronted with widespread textile strikes of a few years before, William Watts Ball, the choleric Charleston editor, seriously proposed

83

limiting the ballot to the literate and the property owner. One of the anomalies of very recent southern scholarship is that the history of the blacks is being meticulously covered, but little attention has been paid to the economically deprived white classes. Even a superficial study of the depiction of the poor white character in the southern novel during the first half of this century will indicate what meaning the literate southerner placed upon the word *community*. Throughout the scope of southern literature, from Ellen Glasgow to William Faulkner and beyond, there are many understanding and sympathetic studies of Negro characters, and although fewer, some such characterizations of the yeoman farmer, but with the possible exception of the mountain breed, and for the period of the Great Depression, little has been written about the poor white except in terms of disdain and ridicule.

In a very able study of the recent South, Thomas D. Clark has ventured the opinion that the power of the old southern oligarchy, challenged by the rise of a large urban middle class, is seemingly on the decline. This should be true. But if so, the new forces have yet to effect any substantial change in the relative wage rates of the region's industrial workers. Payments by the federal government for such items as unemployment, relief, medical care, and education, particularly where such programs have not been directly administered by local politicians, have, of course, given a sizable thrust to the rise of the section's poor, whether white or black. The very recent, vastly improved employment opportunities for Negroes is undeniable. But official statistics of 1969 indicated that the lowest average wage rates in the country were to be found in Mississippi, one of the more conservative and least industrialized of southern states, and in North Carolina, one of the more progressive and industrialized, now ranking twelfth among all American states in the value of its manufactured products. By amount of wages paid per hour, Mississippi ranked forty-ninth among the fifty states, North Carolina, fiftieth. In the light of such statistics one is forced to wonder whether U. B. Phillips' quintessential statement about the mentality of the antebellum South should not be amended, for the twentieth century, whether Phillips' reported common resolve that the South "shall be and remain a white man's country" should not read "an upper-class white man's country."

Much unmistakable evidence exists, of course, that the position and power of the southern oligarchy has been materially reduced during the very recent past. Both the insistence on the maintenance of racial barriers and differentials in wages, relief payments, and other social services helped to induce a massive flow of blacks to the North during the past thirty years. That migration, along with a complex of other factors, has so changed the nature of the national Democratic Party that it has long ceased to be a congenial haven for the average upper-class southerner. Since President Truman's establishment of a permanent Civil Rights Commission and his subsequent enunciation of the Fair Deal, the waxing power of labor and the liberal-Negro coalition among the northern Democrats has increasingly disenchanted the conservative. The welter of local and regional "Democratic Parties" whose qualified names indicated their opposition to the national organization, together with sizable defections to the Republicans, reveal the extent of his frustration with national politics. And the growing inclination of the rapidly rising urban vote in the South to react as northern city voters do has compounded his unease.

Now after fifteen years of civil rights decisions and acts and massive federal expenditures for the poor, it would seem that the southern conservatives' fifty-year trade-off has been disastrous for their most cherished causes, that their willingness to support the making of the present social service nation in return for being permitted to fashion a racial and labor policy within the boundaries of their own section, contained such paradoxes that the agreement was bound to eventuate in their ultimate defeat, and thus provide another footnote to the historical process as being one in which myopic statesmen lead blind masses into an opaque future.

But such a judgment is only a partial one limited to the immediate present and one which comprehends neither the extent of the conservative's personal success over the years nor his impact upon federal and regional policy. Viewed from his own peculiar angle of values, the southern conservative, even as late as 1970, could point to the following achievements: He has consistently managed to dominate a Congressional party structure in which he has been as much a minority in Congress as among the voters of the party to which he nominally belongs. At the opening of the Ninety-first Congress in January, 1969, twelve of the sixteen standing committees of the Senate were chaired by southerners, of which only one could have conceivably been called a liberal on matters of race and labor policy—Ralph W. Yarborough of Texas, who was subsequently defeated. In the House where the power of an urban-centered coalition of ethnic groups, laborers, liberals, and social welfareites was much more concentrated, eleven of the twenty standing committees were chaired by southerners of traditional views.

Whether the southern conservative in the future could retain his privileged position in the House of

Representatives and the Senate is questionable, the outcome depending upon a number of complicated political equations, including the major one hinging upon the viability of the Democrats as the majority party throughout the South. The 1968 success of President Nixon's southern strategy throughout the upper South may well spread downward to include Congressional contests and laterally to the rest of the section. In that case, the southern conservative, allied in name as well as in principle to the Republicans of the northern suburbs and of the western Middle West, may temporarily lose power in the Congressional committee structure while over the long run gaining it for his social and political values.

The southern conservative position on labor unions and wage floor policies has been under general attack for some time. Change may be imminent in the ranks of public employees as well as those of the factory and mercantile houses located in the more urban regions of the section. But in 1971 the southern wage differential persisted, the right to work laws were still on the books, and organized labor could still refer to the South as the Siberia of the labor movement.

The future of the American labor movement both North and South may partially depend upon the intensity of racial tensions in the two sections. For mass urbanization of blacks carries its divisive threat to union labor as well as to the old configuration of the Democratic Party. And while the George Wallace movement connecting white racism with reform may for a time, as in the Progressive era, strengthen the possibility for liberal action to benefit the white sector, over the longer run, as in the past, rising racial tension will probably only intensify the conservative position on both racial and nonracial matters.

Certainly the southern conservatives' cherished racial policies have been overturned, supported, ironically, from the conservative viewpoint, by a southern Democratic President. But subsequently the southern conservative lived to see a great many northerners, by their acts if not always by their professions, espouse some of his racial views, and a succeeding Republican President virtually accept the essence of Senator James F. Byrnes's 1938 "southern strategy." In substituting "Middle America" for "the Great Society," Richard Nixon fashioned his appeal to a geographical as well as an economic, social, and racial formula. The South responded in the 1968 elections with five of the Old Confederate states voting for the Republican and only one for the Democrat Hubert Humphrey, a result almost identical to that in the western Middle West where the margin ran six to one for the Republican. Allowing for the possible distortions of votes cast for George Wallace in the South and on the basis of the Viet Nam War issue in both regions, the sectional pattern is similar enough to support, somewhat, the more broadly based social analysis in the first chapter.

Finally, I would submit that the seventy-year performance of the group of southern conservatives we have considered is one of the most remarkable in the history of so-called democratic politics. It is a tale of a minority political and social group within their national party and perhaps within their own section, consistently voicing minority opinions about two transcendent areas in American life, who not only maintained themselves in their states and in Washington, but sustained much of the substance, if not the legal forms, of their social creed. As such, the record attests to the persistent power of the southern elite in the past and suggests a continued vitality in the future.